Copyright © 2023
make believe ideas ltd

The Wilderness, Berkhamsted, Hertfordshire, HP4 2AZ, UK.
6th Fl., South Bank House, Barrow St., Dublin 4, D04 TR29, Ireland.

All rights reserved. No part of this publication may be reproduced, stored in a retrieval system, or transmitted in any form or by any means, electronic, mechanical, photocopying, recording, or otherwise, without the prior written permission of the copyright owner.

www.makebelieveideas.co.uk
Written by Holly Lansley.
Illustrated by Beverley Hopwood.

The Unbelievable TRUTH about... SANTA

Beverley Hopwood · Holly Lansley

make believe ideas

Santa Claus is known worldwide for spreading **CHRISTMAS CHEER,** but no one knows exactly how he gets it **DONE** each year.

Next, they say that Santa Claus arrives by **FIREPLACE**. But not all homes have chimneys, so that **CANNOT** be the case.

Really, it's his **REINDEER SQUAD** who look at every home...

then **work out** how to get **inside WITHOUT** it being known.

Inside, instead of COOKIES, it's the CARROTS Santa eats. They help him with his eyesight,

And **no one** knows that Santa's **SUITS** should all be **WHITE** instead.

But he **washed** them with some **UNDERPANTS...**

The REAL reason he keeps a LIST, and always checks it TWICE,

'Cause, Santa would **forget** his hat without his **trusted TEAM**.

OPERATION SECRET SANTA
SLEIGH 8 × REINDEER

They **help** him make sure Christmas always runs just like a **DREAM**.

In fact, it was the **elves** who got **fed up** with all the **snow**.

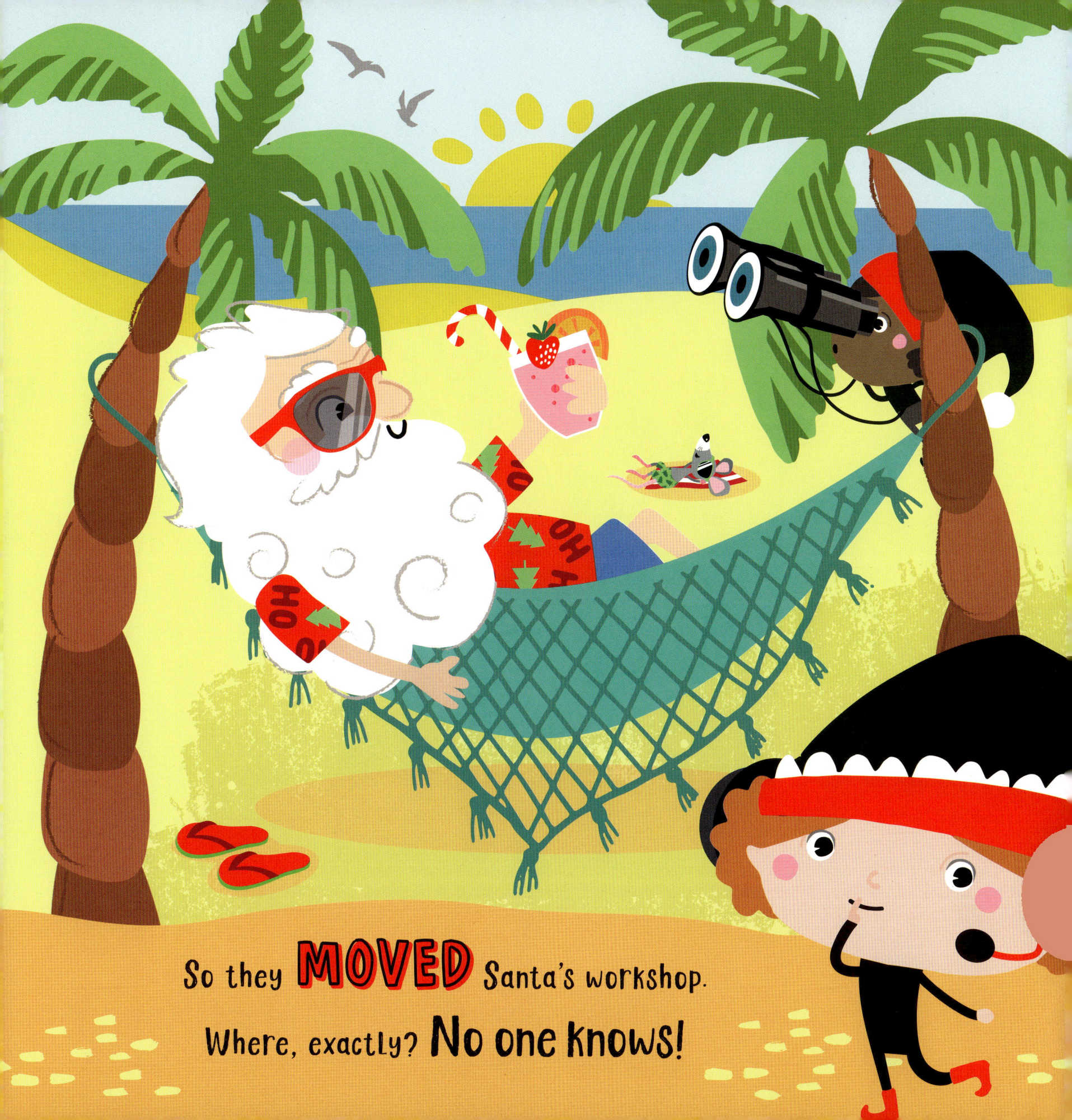

So they MOVED Santa's workshop. Where, exactly? No one knows!

His sleigh can WHIZZ through TIME AND SPACE in one FANTASTIC flight.

So, now you know the JOLLY TRUTH, but don't you ever fear:

Santa Claus can't wait to spread his MAGIC every year!